The first four years

of adulthood

Table of Contents

14. Chapter 12 KEEP GROWIN

FOREWORD

Im no expert on being and adult. I am not the perfect adult. I have made many mistakes throughout my journey of adulthood. So, I am not claiming to be the cleanest towel in the house nor am I claiming to be the sharpest tool in the shed. But with all of my mistakes I have learned and now understand how to get positive results in life. But what works for me may not work for you because I am just another human being on the journey, we call life.

ABOUT THE AUTHOR

My story starts in Jacksonville Florida at University hospital.

July 1,1980, I gasp my first breath of this formidable filthy loving hateful beautiful cruel exciting selfish giving GOD fearing no faith having faithful deceitful air in a world that I believe is whatever you make it. Then I died three times nah for real.

I was a pre mature baby that died 3 times after I woke on the 3rd time I was placed in a incubator and oddly enough I remember being in that plastic container bubble crib house or whatever they call it I also remember having needles and tubes everywhere but that's all I remember but those memories are vivid.

My mother was 30 and my father was 46. Awesome people in my opinion. As a child I was very active and fat do not ask ion know how that works but hey it worked. We moved a lot not by choice but by bad habits, bad decisions and circumstance meaning we were evicted a lot,hold up rewind let me clear my dad's name. I lived with my mom during the week and my dad and grandma on most weekends so I had two separate sets of friends one on the Northside (which my grandma and dad never moved and were pretty much stable and a different set of friends and standards also across the bridge on the Southside/Brookview / Ft. Caroline/ Parental Home/ Regency area hey I said we moved a lot but mostly we lived in brookview area. So, I was blessed to experience two different lifestyles.

In school I was somewhat of a class clown / trouble maker I guess that's why I was 15 in the 6th grade I wasn't dumb I was just very Mischievous doing things that I wouldn't recommend for example me and a few friends started our own gang some of us sold weed but we all were definitely outside, we would smoke weed every day we didn't really bother anyone and no one bothered us, too often but it's not because we were tough it was because they had older brothers and I had older cousins that everybody new didn't play about us and they would take it there if anyone played with us or them so we were pretty protected in that manner but we did our share of dirt too and thankful it didn't cost me the reason I say it didn't cost me was because I eventually got on track passed the necessary tests and met the requirements to be skipped to my correct grade so I didn't experience 7th 8th 9th or tenth grade yea you guessed it ,I went from 6th to 11th grade and graduated at 17 with my correct class the class of 98' although it wasn't a traditional high school it was a trade school so along the way I picked up a brick mason certificate escaped being a statistic didn't go to jail or juvenile didn't die in the streets and I graduated. To get to the graduation point ,In between all of that as a teenager from 12-17 I worked with the student work program where I went door to door and business to business selling candy and such items. I was real good at it so good in fact I was the top seller most nights and weekends earning around $50 per night and between $150 $200 on weekends(including donations that we were not supposed to take) Also the Guy that was our boss would pick me up early and take me to restock boxes he would pay me like a extra $250-$300 per week to stock the candy boxes during the week. We still talk to this day. I learned a lot from him, he was the one that really showed me that you can get money and set your own pay and do it all legally. He would not admit it but to me he was rich, and I wanted to be rich too.

I was making enough money to help my mom with some bills I was able to purchase my own clothes and shoes by age 12 to take that burden off moms. But everything was not all good all the time we still had some ghetto experiences our lights and water were disconnected often I remember I had to go down the street to my girlfriend's house to fill water jugs so that we could flush our toilet.

My mom had a few different boyfriend's during my childhood so I picked up different things from different men and my grandma made sure everyone understood that you only have one dad and it was no such thing as a step dad because my dad was actually in my life and active until he died.I was 17 when he died and guess who found him behind the couch lifeless yea lucky me. But the way GOD works is amazing that night before I went to bed me and my dad stayed up and talked for hours he told me his life stories he even told me about when he was a drug dealer and how he use to go out to Miami and would have certain woman traffic the drugs in their body parts how he stared popping pills which led to stronger drugs and got addicted and how as a youngster he held his brother over a balcony during a fight, how his dad was not present he told of times when he was married and some of his infidelities , but don't twist my story he was a great dad and if you didn't know him you would not know he used drugs he wasn't a typical user, stealing killing begging and being funky and embarrassing naw he was the exact opposite of all that even though he knew, I had money not one time ever did he ask me for money or even take money from me.

He made sure i had everything that I needed when i was with him he rarely cursed or raised his voice he smoked cigarettes but never in front of me, I may have seen him drink some crown one time so erase that awful picture that you painted of my dad in your head and start over with the real picture.

I felt the need to clear that up back to the story.

That night he told me everything and some stuff he made me promise not to repeat now what's is even stranger is he gave me a half bag of Cheeto's and all of his money (He had just gotten his disability check) He had never done this before.

I know what he did and who he did it with. As a matter of fact ,I looked up to the guys that sold him the drugs they treated my like a lil brother they would come pick me up give me money make sure I went to school even take me to school, they would tell me their story's of how they came into the life of selling drugs and how one day they would do something different and how they better never catch me doing what they were doing and to play sports and be a kid and respect adults all the things that big brothers are supposed to tell lil brothers and they protected me as well.

Back to the story, my dad would stay up for days him and his associates in the garage in our backyard.

Needless to say, he did not make my graduation(HE DIED remember)in which I had to ride the city bus to in full cap and gown. I did not mention that in 11th and 12th grade I stayed full time with my dad and grandma. I played organized sports my senior year only.

Now on the other side of the bridge was different but a lot of similarities.

Drugs were involved I witnessed crack being cooked in the microwave. Bodies were falling and lots of people were given lots of time in jail. My mom was friends with what I believe to be drug kingpins of my childhood,

Let's just say when they got busted it was national news, and it was connected from south America thru Florida to Texas and so on. So, they definitely deserve a documentary.

I remember staying at their house and the rooms were packed full with all kinds of stuff from trading cards to electronics to whatever you can think of that had value because the drug attics would pawn these things for drugs so of course I wanted to be a drug kingpin because these things were present in my everyday life on both sides of the bridge. Unbelievably in my experience drug dealers were some of the most caring people that I have ever been around, and they did not try to get us kids involved, they would steer us in the opposite direction. But when you see what we saw and experience what we did it became a norm and something that I wanted to become and I truly believe if I didn't take that bet back in 12th grade during my brick mason class when me and a friend were shooting dice I would be a king pin now.

O you are wondering what bet well I'm glad you asked. On this particular day we had guests, some guys from the army that set up a trailer on the school site, and they were signing kids up for the military and my friend bet me $5 that I would not go in the trailer and sign up. Back then if I was challenged, I'm going to prove that I wasn't scared of anything so I went and signed up came out the trailer got my $5 and in less than 2 minutes lost my $5 shooting dice but that would prove to be the best decision in my life up until that point.

It was a quick transition. I graduated June 98' turned 18 July 98' got shipped off to basic training August 98' FT. Benning Ga, home of the infantry once basic was over I was stationed in Ft. Campbell Ky where I began to learn how to become a Black man in America. I won't tell this story in this book but if I decide to share that story it was an awesome time filled with fun ,deployments, near death experiences,lots of protected sex,alcohol,drugs,sin,bad decisions ,new friendships ,lessons learned and whole lot of good clean fun. After I served my 9 years, I received an honorable discharge. Met my beautiful wife in the process and helped contribute to producing 4 wonderful kids or at least I think so most of the time. They have been blessed to live a wonderful life compared to the way I was raised. But do not twist the story I would not change any chapter in my life. Maybe a sentence or two but definitely not a chapter. But enough about me let's get to what we came here for.

Chapter 1

LISTEN MORE THAN YOU TALK AND ALWAYS DO YOUR RESEARCH

When I say listen more than you talk, listening shows emotional intelligence. Listening also helps you understand others' perspectives, needs, and emotions. You are less likely to jump to conclusions or misinterpret situations.

One of the many lessons that I was taught by my mother's fiancé and something that I live by today is he would often tell me before you say anything out loud say it twice in your head. My interpretation was if it is not helpful or a solution or something relevant do not say it. Another take away is its always necessary to be careful what you say and who you say it too.

I have also learned that when people feel heard, they feel valued and sometimes it deepens that relationship whether personal or professional. I take it as a valuable opportunity with every conversation, no matter with who or no matter the subject it is a chance to gain new knowledge or see things from a perspective other than my own.

Talking also reaffirms what we already know, while listening expands our understanding. Most times all it takes is understanding to solve problems and conflicts. I have learned what most conflicts have in common is that there is not a clear understanding. The only way to have a clear understanding is through communication which the major part is listening to understand what the other party is trying to translate.

Also listening can de-escalate tension. Most of the time people just want to be heard. It helps uncover root issues, rather than just getting a reaction. The best leaders listen first. They gather input, to make more informed decisions. Listening makes others more receptive to your ideas when it is your turn to speak. Most communication breakdowns come from not truly listening basically hearing only part of what was said or interpreting it based on assumptions.

In a noisy world where everyone wants to talk, genuine listening is a rare gift. It sets you apart. But nevertheless, after listening always do your research because people will tell you anything or they will tell the part that looks or sounds good. So, it is up to you to seek the knowledge and find the truth. Remember it is always 3 sides to a story their side your side and what actually happened.

After all, if you look in the mirror **GOD** gave most of us two ears and one mouth for a reason right. Speaking of **GOD** that takes us to chapter 2.

Chapter 2

HAVE FAITH IN A HIGHER POWER

To be honest this is a personal choice, and everyone will not agree but I think everyone believes in something to some degree ok, not everyone but the vast majority of humanity.

For me belief in a higher power does not mean you or I understand why we exist or what our lives are for. But to some it provides a framework to understand suffering, joy, and our place in the universe and a moral compass/guide for what is right and wrong.

In times of hardship or uncertainty, we may find strength in the idea that a greater presence is watching over us. Also, it gives some of us hope that things will swing in our favor if we keep pushing forward and may help some of us not give up on ourselves and each other. For others it may give us something to look forward to and strive to make us better human beings.

It can bring comfort during grief, illness, or major life transitions.

But for me the most important thing is believing in a higher power gives us ethical guidelines along with compassion, justice, humility, forgiveness, a guide to how we treat each other.

Others find belief in a higher power allows them to connect with something beyond material existence. It can inspire humility, give a deeper appreciation for life and nature.

But with all of that we still are human and sometimes we have doubts. For most curiosity is part of a thoughtful spiritual journey.

Some people say they find meaning without belief in a higher power through philosophy, humanism, science, or relationships. (BUT THAT ALL KIND OF MEANS YOU BELIEVE IN SOMETHING BECAUSE IF YOU DIDN'T THEN HOW WOULD YOU GAUGE WHATS RIGHT WRONG OR GOOD AND BAD. BELIEF IS ESSENTIALLY OUR MORAL COMPASS)

For me believing in a higher power does not always mean subscribing to a specific religion.

While we have this topic fresh on our mind and it has been taught to us that forgiveness is powerful and if you are a believer then you understand without forgiveness, we do not get the ultimate promise.

You must also understand that while it is mandatory to **FORGIVE BUT NECESSARY TO NNNNNNNNEVERRRRRRRRRRR FORGET**

Chapter 3

FORGIVE BUT DONT FORGET

In life we all have done things that we meant to be good, but things turned out bad, and on the outside, it looked like we did something purposely that hurt or offended someone that we had no intention of making feel that way. So, with that in mind we must go back to understanding that communication is the root of misunderstandings. Me personally around 2009, I began to believe in my heart that I overcame people, meaning that from that point on, I understood that people were not perfect and that people will disappoint you even the ones that you think are the closest will do things that you would never think they would do, but we have all done things that we want no one to ever find out about. After all we are imperfect humans and sometimes that human instinct kicks in and our moral compass shuts off. For many varied reasons and who are we to judge what is valid, because if we are in a certain situation who is to say how we would handle it. When people's backs are against the wall and the pressure is building up, maybe it is a once in a lifetime opportunity to get them out of a bind should we be loyal to ourselves /situation or to someone else and their situation. All these things become factors and must be considered when you feel like someone wronged you.

At this point I truly understood that humans are not perfect so to expect anything more than that is ridiculous. Us as people do things that we normally would not want others. Realizing that situations put people in positions sometimes where it feels like the only way out is too do something that they feel is necessary to ease the burden, and sometimes the pain, hoping that the deed is never revealed, because it will cause more pain than the original situation.

Other times people do things as acts of revenge for things others may have done or even a simple misunderstanding because instead of listening more, they choose to talk more and do not listen to understand.

So with me understanding these things I have learned not to judge others,while not putting faith in and never to fully trust others but in the mist of all of that it's imperative that I forgive others because who am I to not forgive others when I can't say I honestly knew there intentions, with that being said I may have forgiven someone but I won't forget what they did or how it made me feel. So, from the point of forgiveness, I will do my best to not let myself be put in that position again by that person to violate my trust again. Some may say that I am not truly forgiving but I am reminded of what a friend told me once. We cannot choose the punishment that someone feels we deserve for wronging them because what may seem to be the perfect penalty for you may not cover the cost for the offended person.

For me forgiveness brings a sense of peace. Once you have that peace you learn to let things play out because normally the outcome you have in your head is not close to the true outcome of letting things play out

So sometimes you must <u>LET THINGS PLAY OUT</u>

Chapter 4

Let things play out!

This is a big one here it takes a lot of discipline and patience but to get through the process you must understand moving to fast or assuming (ASS U ME) makes a ass out of you and me as I was often told when I was younger.

For me this means that you do not know what I am thinking, and I do not know what you are thinking so instead of assuming and rushing to get a result just be patient and let things play out. More times than not you will be surprised that the outcome is vastly different from what you imagined in your mind.

The reason I say this is because if you don't let things play out and rush for answers or results then you may not get a genuine result. People can say well I was not going to do this or that when in reality it's exactly what they planned but they did not expect you to catch them in their bullcrap. Here are a few things to keep in mind.

Assumptions distort reality When you assume, you are filling in blanks with your own expectations, fears, or biases. That can create misunderstandings or unnecessary stress.

Life is unpredictable Outcomes often turn out differently than we imagine. By waiting, you give reality the chance to show itself instead of reacting to a false version of events.

Avoids conflict Acting on assumptions can damage relationships, because you might treat someone unfairly based on what you **think** is happening instead of what is true.

Keeps you open-minded

Letting things unfold builds patience and helps you stay flexible, which makes it easier to adapt to whatever happens.

Protects your peace Assuming the worst can cause unnecessary anxiety. Letting things play out keeps you calmer and more grounded in the present moment.

Builds trust in the process Sometimes the best insights, solutions, and outcomes only appear with time. Allowing events to develop naturally often leads to better results than forcing conclusions.

So always remember that assumptions close doors; patience keeps them open.

Chapter 5

DON'T THROW ROCKS IN A GLASS HOUSE!!

That can cover so much as it relates to us as humans. For me it is something that I try to live by. I know I'm not the greatest human being in the eyes of some people. Everyone has a different view. But when I meet people or have conversations with people, I never judge them based off what someone else told me about them,now if someone tells me about a person then it's smart to be remember what was said but never make that the main focus simply because circumstances and life will put you in some tough positions and you will have to make decisions that you never thought you would make. The way life is set up you can never say what you will or will not do until you are put in the situation and boom you are doing what you judged someone else for doing. When this happens you now become a hypocrite. An simple example you could criticize someone for being late 4 times in one week but you may not know the circumstances of why you just quickly placed judgement and now are gossiping about said person and as karma has it the following week you are late for something for a reason that you believe to be valid furthermore you find out that they are now gossiping about you and you become angry with them for doing the exact same thing that you did. This is apart of over coming people. But more importantly <u>**BE CAREFUL WHAT YOU SAY WHO YOU SAY IT ABOUT AND WHO YOU SAY IT TOO**</u>

Chapter 6

BE CAREFUL WHAT YOU SAY WHO YOU SAY IT TO AND WHO YOU SAY IT ABOUT

We all know the saying it is a small world and that becomes more evident the older you get the more people you meet the more places you travel the more events you attend.

Let us pause for a second because that higher power we discussed earlier every so often gives me a message for you. It was right when I said, **"<u>THE MORE EVENTS YOU ATTEND."</u>** The message in that message is you do not have to be on every scene or at every event.

In life the less you show up the more important your presence is when you grace the place. So, focus on the mission and the main things and every so often you can show up and watch how much your presence is appreciated.

What we sometimes as humans do not
always understand is the places that you go
often influence who you become also being
at the wrong place at the wrong time can put
you in situations that are extremely
uncomfortable or dangerous.

You some invites that are out of convenience,
expectation, or even for them to use you, not
out of genuine care.

Most importantly saying yes, every time can sometimes leave you drained and if you are always going or doing something when asked it is a 98.4% chance that you are neglecting something that you should not. In short, saying no more often than yes helps you keep balance and helps keep you focused on the things in your life that complete you this may also help keep you less stressed.

OK BACK TO THE SUBJECT!!!!

As we all know words can't be taken back no matter how mad or drunk or high or whatever state of mind you were in once spoken they are forever etched in whoever you spoke them to mind and depending on the person and the way the message is interpreted they those words will spread quickly, and more often than not be twisted.

Saying the wrong thing to the wrong person at the wrong time can damage how others see you, sometimes permanently. Some people may use your words against you, gossip about you, or misrepresent what you said. careless words can hurt feelings, cause conflict, or create misunderstandings.

As I said in an earlier chapter, UNDERSTANDING is the most important part when relaying a message to others because what feels fine to say in private with a close friend might be inappropriate, risky, or misunderstood in public or professional settings.

It is also important to remember the world is small and more people are connected than we sometimes realize so the wrong word in the workplace, for example, might affect promotions, teamwork, or networking. In school and in general people know people that you never thought they would know. A personal experience that I had in my past takes me back to my early 20's, I was at my first official duty station in Ft. Campbell Ky. The back story goes like this I had been dating a certain young lady for a few months, So one day she has one of her close female friends call my phone with her on the phone as well apparently I didn't want to talk to her that day is why I didn't answer when she called but that's a story for another book. Well after the conversation was over between the 3 of us I asked the question "why would you have another female call my phone, her response was it doesn't matter because she is not your type, well what she didn't know was the female that she had call me was the first female that I dated when I arrived to Ft. Campbell and we lost contact because I did a tour overseas and when I came back, I lost contact information. So long story short she doubled back and called me once she was off the phone with her friend. Needless to say, she was still my type. My point remains you never know who knows who or how close they are or once were.

Remember words have power, and once they are out, you cannot control where they go or how they are received. This way you protect yourself and your reputation.

Chapter 7

All you have in this world.

Your word is your reputation, your word is your character, your word is your credibility. Whenever you say something, do it good or bad. Stand on what you say to the best of your ability. Rather than switching up when it is time to cash the check that your mouth wrote just follow through and let things play out and you may be surprised with the outcome. A lot of the relationships that I have built were structured because 96% of the time if I say something I'm going to do everything in my power to follow through now in some cases it's out of my control but even if I have to take a loss or the final result is not in my favor I still follow through because my reputation is so important to me .In most cases your reputation is built off of the things that you do and say if you say things and don't follow through that will become how people view you. Now I know a lot of us were raised to not care what others think about us but that is completely false. Perception is important to us even if we don't admit it. Im not saying that we should try to impress everyone but in certain situations we want to shine and look good. The only thing in this world that we have is our word.

So do not be a person that cannot be depended on.

Chapter 8

PROTECT YOUR PEACE

Peace is one of the most valuable things you can hold on to in your adult years. Protecting your peace does not mean avoiding responsibility or living in a bubble. It means being intentional about what you allow into your life whether that's people, places, habits, or even your own thoughts.

The reality is life is already hard enough without inviting unnecessary stress. There will always be drama, conflict, and negativity. But adulthood is when you begin to understand that not every battle deserves your energy, and not every situation deserves your reaction. Maturity is knowing when to speak and when to stay silent, when to walk away and when to stand your ground.

Protecting your peace might mean saying

"no" more often. It might mean cutting ties with old friendships that are no longer healthy. It might even mean creating boundaries with your family, and that is never easy. But boundaries are not walls, they are fences with gates, designed to keep you safe while still letting in what is good for you. When I was in my early twenties, I used to think I had to be everywhere, do everything. I answered every call and got involved in things that did not even concern me.

What it did was rob me of my focus. I was distracted and constantly caught in other people's mess. One day, I realized that I was not even fighting my own battles. From then on, I decided if it does not protect my peace, it is not worth it. Peace is tied to focus. Without peace, your mind is scattered.

Without focus, your goals are delayed. Think about it, have you ever tried to work on a goal while being stressed out or surrounded by negativity? It is almost impossible. Protecting your peace is protecting your future. Here is the truth, not everything needs a response. Sometimes silence is the best reply. Sometimes walking away is the strongest move. And sometimes protecting your peace looks like letting people believe what they want to believe, even if it is not true, because you know the truth does not need defending it reveals itself with time. So, as you grow into adulthood, ask yourself one simple question before you react: "Is this worth my peace?" If the answer is no, then let it go. That choice alone will save you years of wasted time, energy, and stress.

Chapter 9

LEAVE SOMETHING BEHIND

Adulthood is more than bills, jobs, and responsibilities it is about building something that lasts beyond you.
Legacy is not always about money, property, or fame. Sometimes it is about the little things you teach your kids, the kindness you show a stranger, or the way people feel after they have been around you. Those small moments stack up and become the memory of who you were. Every decision you make today is shaping your legacy. Your reputation is part of it, your words are part of it, and your actions are the biggest part of it. People may forget what you owned or what you drove, but they will never forget how you treated them or made them feel. They will never forget your character, I remember

being young and seeing how certain people in my neighborhood were remembered. Some were known for their generosity. Some were remembered for the way they helped others even when they had little themselves. And some were remembered for destruction ,broken promises, lies, or pain they caused. The truth is, we do not get to control how others treat us, leaving something behind also means creating opportunities for others. Whether it is your children, your friends, or even strangers, your effort today can make life easier for someone tomorrow. Think about the doors someone else opened for you, teachers, mentors, family, or even a stranger who believed in you. Part of your job in adulthood is to keep that cycle going. The first four years of adulthood are when you start laying the foundation. These years might not define your entire legacy, but they shape the direction. Start with your word, with your character, with your choices. Because at the end of the day, your legacy will not be built on what you had it will be built on what you gave. Always remember your words, your peace, and your legacy are the three things no one can take from you unless you give them away.

Chapter 10

DISCIPLINE OVER MOTIVATION

Motivation is temporary. It is a spark, not a fire. And if you rely only on motivation, you will never be consistent in adulthood. Motivation might get you started, but discipline is what keeps you going. There were mornings in the military when I woke up exhausted and sore. Motivation did not get me out of bed. Discipline did. Discipline is doing what you said you would do, long after the feeling that made you say it has passed. It is the routine, the habit, the commitment to the goal regardless of how you feel in the moment. Think about fitness. Anyone can be motivated for a week or two. But the ones who change their health are the ones who keep showing up long after motivation disappears. The same goes for money. You might be motivated to save after a big payday, but if you lack discipline, the money slips right through your hands,and in relationships, motivation might bring excitement at the start, but discipline is what keeps you loyal, patient, and present when things get tough. The truth is that most people lose because they are waiting to "feel like it." Successful people win because they do it whether they feel like it or not. Discipline is the bridge between goals and results. If you want to succeed in adulthood, build habits that do not depend on emotion. Build routines that you can follow on good days and bad days. Let motivation inspire you but let discipline carry you. Motivation starts the fire, but discipline keeps it burning.

Chapter 11

CHOOSE YOUR CIRCLE WISELY

Your circle will either push you forward or pull you back. The people you surround yourself with shape your thoughts, your habits, and even your future. That is why choosing your circle wisely is one of the most important decisions you will ever make in adulthood. Not everyone who grew up with you is meant to grow with you. Some people are only in your life for a season. Some are there to teach you lessons, and some are there to hold you back. The sooner you recognize the difference, the better off you will be. I have seen people lose opportunities because they stayed loyal to the wrong circle. I have also seen people elevate their entire lives simply because they surrounded themselves with driven, positive people.

Energy is contagious. If you hang around people who complain, gossip, and make excuses, it will not be long before you start doing the same. But if you are around people who work hard, stay focused, and chase their goals, that energy will rub off on you too. Sometimes protecting your circle means being alone for a while until you find the right people. Loneliness is better than bad company. A small circle of people who genuinely want to see you win is more valuable than a crowd of so called friends who only come around when it benefits them. So, choose wisely. Your circle reflects your future.

Chapter 12

HANDLE YOUR BUSINESS

Adulthood comes with freedom, but freedom without responsibility turns into chaos. Handling your business is about doing what needs to be done on time, without excuses. It is about taking ownership of your life and not waiting for someone else to clean up your mess. When bills are due, pay them. If you owe someone pay them.When you make a commitment, follow through. When you set a goal, pursue it with consistency. Handling your business does not mean you will not make mistakes, it means you will not hide from them. It means you face challenges head on and keep moving forward. One lesson I learned early in adulthood was that excuses do not pay bills. Complaining does not fix problems. Excuses do not impress employers or landlords. Results do. That's why I created the slogan

"NO EXCUSES JUST RESULTS"

People respect effort, accountability, and reliability. Thats how you build trust, and trust opens doors. When you handle your business, you separate yourself from the crowd. People notice. Opportunities show up. And most importantly, you start to build confidence in yourself. You begin to realize that you do not have to wait on anyone else, you can take care of your responsibilities and creating a future you can be proud of. So, no matter what comes your way, stand on your word, handle your business, and watch how life begins to reward you.

Chapter 13

KEEP GROWING

One of the worst mistakes you can make in adulthood is believing that you've "arrived." The truth is that growth is lifelong. The moment you stop learning; you start falling behind. Growth is what keeps you sharp, adaptable, and prepared for the change life will always bring. The first four years of adulthood are only the foundation. From there, every stage of life introduces new lessons. Some lessons are painful like losing someone you love, failing at a job, or going through tough financial situations. Others are rewarding like finding your passion, achieving a goal, or starting a family. But all of them shape you. Growth does not always mean degrees, promotions, or money. Sometimes growth is internal learning, patience, gaining wisdom, or becoming more disciplined. Sometimes it is learning to walk away, to forgive yourself, or to stand firm in your values. Growth happens in the little decisions you make daily, not just the big milestones. Never let success make you lazy. Never let failure make you quit. Keep reading. Keep asking questions. Keep looking for better. Surround yourself with people who challenge you to rise higher. Step outside your comfort zone because comfort is where dreams go to die. At the end of the day, adulthood is not about being perfect, it is about being better today than you were yesterday. Keep growing, because the moment you stop learning, you stop living.

Thanks for reading. My hope is that you were able to grab something and apply it to your life. The wording and inconsistency of the way the book was presented was done to show that even when you think everything must be perfect that even with imperfections your message can still be received.

Thanks to everyone that supported me and thanks to A.I for the book cover.

Made in the USA
Middletown, DE
07 January 2026

24032570R00050